How to Be Your Child's Best College Coach

Strategies for Success Using Teens You'll Find Lying Around the House

Lee Binz

The HomeScholar

First Printing, 2018

Printed in the United States of America

Cover Design by Robin Montoya
Edited by Kimberly Charron

ISBN: 9781731481023

Disclaimer: Parents assume full responsibility for the education of their children in accordance with state law. College requirements vary, so make sure to check with the colleges about specific requirements for homeschoolers. We offer no guarantees, written or implied, that the use of our products and services will result in college admissions or scholarship awards.

How to Be Your Child's Best College Coach

Strategies for Success Using Teens You'll Find Lying Around the House

What are Coffee Break Books?

How to Be Your Child's Best College Coach is part of The HomeScholar's Coffee Break Book series.

Designed especially for parents who don't want to spend hours and hours reading a 400-page book on homeschooling high school, each book combines Lee's practical and friendly approach with detailed, but easy-to-digest information, perfect to read over a cup of coffee at your favorite coffee shop!

Never overwhelming, always accessible and manageable, each book in the series will give parents the tools they need to tackle the tasks of homeschooling high school, one warm sip at a time.

Everything about these Coffee Break Books is designed to suggest simplicity, ease and comfort – from the size (fits in a purse), to the font and paragraph length (easy on the eyes), to the price (the same as a Starbucks Venti Triple Caramel Macchiato). Unlike a fancy coffee drink, however, these books are guilt-free pleasures you will want to enjoy again and again!

Table of Contents

Introduction

Homeschooling's Red Light Camera

The college launch is when you launch your sweet child into life – the real world – after homeschooling. So, it is the culmination of your child's homeschool preparation. In this book, *launch* refers primarily to the launch into college, but can also mean your child's launch into career or trade school.

While this book is written for homeschool families, parents of public and private school students will also find helpful information to supplement the guidance counselor advice their teens may (or, more likely, may not) be getting in high school.

You know those red light cameras in big cities? They snap pictures when you don't stop for the red. You might be 100 percent certain you came to a full and complete stop at the red light . . . until you are confronted with the recording from the red light camera!

In a similar way, you might be 100 percent confident that you and your child are ready for what comes after graduation – but suddenly you are confronted with inadequate college offers that will result in a mountain of debt. Or maybe you will be confronted by an inert mass of humanity lying shiftless and jobless on your couch for six months. This can be like looking at a piece of abstract art entitled "Failure to Launch."

In this book, I'll help you understand all the elements to successfully coach your teen through the concluding act of high school – their graduation. I will teach you the launch sequence, as your child blasts off into adulthood.

Despite what you may have heard, getting into college and earning big scholarships isn't that tricky. You simply need to understand the game and follow simple, proven, logical steps.

I'm glad you are here because this information is important now – long before 12th grade starts – so you know what you need to pay attention to and what is merely noise you can ignore. I'm going to teach you what you need to know and the sequence you should follow for best success.

But first, let me tell you what this book is not. It's **not** a promise of a full scholarship, great riches, or a guarantee of admission to your favorite Ivy league school. But I can promise that you will walk away with a deeper understanding of this critical phase of your parenting career. And I can promise you tools that will let you assess your readiness for the next stage. Parents who understand the launch sequence and take active steps to accomplish these goals will be much further along to help their children achieve their dreams for college and life.

As The HomeScholar, I've been helping parents gain the confidence they need to homeschool from middle school through high school graduation since 2006. I excel at taking complex information and giving it to parents in a way that makes them feel confident and empowered instead of fearful and inadequate. I am proud to be known as "the homeschool consultant who **won't** make you cry." I strive to bring calmness and sanity to my writings and presentations.

By the end of this book, you will know exactly how to be your student's best college coach, including what is involved in a successful college admission result and launch of your young adult. Better still, you will evaluate your readiness for this final chapter of your homeschooling career and honestly assess where you have gaps in your knowledge and might need additional help.

Chapter 1

What is a College Coach?

Before we dive in, I'd like to define terms I will use throughout this book. A *college coach* is a paid professional consultant that can help your teen find colleges, apply, get accepted and earn scholarships. College coaches are different from a term you may be more familiar with – *guidance counselor*.

A guidance counselor is typically a public or private high school employee who is available to guide teens toward a career choice and, as somewhat of an aside, help them with the college admission process. In terms of focus, think of a guidance counselor as a country doctor and a college coach as a heart surgeon. A college coach is typically hired by a teen's parents and usually supports the teen for up to two years, usually junior and senior year of high school. They are highly qualified professionals who also happen to be **extremely expensive**.

While not typically associated with homeschooling, I believe these two roles are critically important for all families of college bound teens. There are a few issues (cost, knowledge, time) which make filling these roles extremely challenging for most families. I will go into great depth about these roles and show how you – the loving parent – are uniquely qualified to fill these roles for your student.

College coaches are a relatively new phenomenon that has gained in popularity as the selectiveness of colleges and competition for big merit scholarships has skyrocketed.

In a nutshell, a college coach is someone who will **trade their expertise in earning college admission and marketing your student for cash.** And they are **not** cheap. The average college coach in the United States charges between $4000 and $6000 to work with your child for a set time between junior and senior year. Some cost much more. I'm not saying they aren't worth the money. They are after all, knowledgeable about hundreds of universities and familiar with many types of college admission requirements across the country. In addition, the better ones have proven themselves able to work with a variety of college applicants and help market them successfully to any college they want to attend.

I would never criticize anyone who trades expertise for cash. It's the same business model for every consultant or coach in the country, including me! What I am painfully aware of, however, is that when we decided to take the homeschooling path, we gave up being a dual income family. When I was homeschooling, we couldn't even begin to think about paying for a year of college, let alone paying an additional $6000 for a college coach! That expense is well out of reach for most families even if both partners are working.

It got me thinking, though . . . the reasons you are the best possible guidance counselor are the same reasons you are your child's best possible college coach.

Think about it for a minute. Everyone understands why a professional coach is necessary to prepare someone to compete in the Olympics. I don't ice skate and I wouldn't understand the difference between figure skating and ice dancing. I am definitely not qualified to coach my child if they aspired for Olympic skating glory.

But getting into college isn't like that! Last time I checked, admission requirements weren't written in Egyptian hieroglyphics and essays weren't required in Latin. Everything college coaches do is in plain old English.

College admission requirements are even written so the average high school student can read and understand them. Sure, fulfilling admission requirements takes work. But it is a **reasonable** amount of work, not an **impossible** amount of work.

Getting back to college coaches . . . you don't need to be knowledgeable about hundreds of universities, do you? And certainly not thousands. When you are coaching your child, you might need some cursory information on perhaps 20 colleges and you probably only need to deeply understand 4 to 12 colleges.

You don't need to understand all the admission requirements in the country but you might need to be familiar with your state colleges and a few private colleges. And you don't need to be able to work with hundreds of different kids you've never met from all socio-economic and capability levels. At most, you need to work with one or two children at a time and you already know them well.

You do know your teen, right? They are more than a number to you.

This is the key. **You should never feel obligated to pay for expertise you don't need.** Most homeschoolers I know get a sense of satisfaction from educating their kids and helping them succeed. That's why most of us homeschool, right? Becoming your child's best possible college coach means learning a few proven strategies and understanding some new terms. It also means working ahead of a well-defined schedule.

You already know and love your kids and have proven up to the task of educating them and preparing them to face adult responsibilities. Why would you think that you can't succeed at launching your kids into college and life?

Chapter 2

College Coaching by the Numbers

478 to 1

Does this ratio mean anything to you? It is the number of high school students per guidance counselor, on average, in the public school system. In many schools, security officers outnumber school counselors!

Those numbers are precisely why, in 2013, 26 percent of all college applicants hired a professional college coach, AKA, *private admissions consultant* or *independent educational consultant* (IEC), to assist with college applications. This number is three times as many as in 2003.

Let's talk about another number. There are approximately 5300 colleges and universities in the United States. A guidance counselor or professional college coach would need to know 5300 colleges well if they can speak authoritatively to any student who hires them.

You see the problem

A college coach can't visit all those colleges, right? No human can know everything about all the colleges and universities in the country. So, what do they do? They research!

There are 13 million students for a college coach to work with. This is roughly the number of 18 to 20-year-olds in the U.S. who a college coach might have as clients. No single human can know about all the universities in the country, as well as 13 million unique individuals. When faced with a new student or a new school to work with, what do they do? Try to get to know them.

Outside the U.S., there are even more students across the globe who want to come into the country to study. College coaches work with at least 80 different countries. Thirty-nine percent of college coaches report they work with "some" international students, and 14 percent say they work with a "significant" number of international students.

How could a college coach keep up? Spoiler alert – they can't. They need to do research. So, let's see how you stack up against a college coach.

The HomeScholar's Official College Coach Qualification Quiz

1. How many students are in your homeschool high school?

2. How many adults guide the high school students in your home?

3. How many universities will your student apply to? (Hint: typically, four to eight)

4. On a scale of one to ten, how well do you know these children? (One means you can't place a name with the face and ten means they are probably laying on your couch right now.)

For many students, the high school guidance counselor is the only college coach they have. I'll tell you a secret – only 4 out of 10 public school students ever speak to their guidance counselor. **On average, a public school guidance counselor will spend 38 minutes per student over the course of a 4-year high school career.**

{Dramatic pause to let this sink in . . .}

So, how much time did you spend with your child today? You see, even if you are half as good as a college coach, you can be hundreds of times more effective. You are more than enough to be the guidance counselor.

One homeschooler wrote to me about her experience:

> *We hired a college coach, I feel she was totally off the mark with her suggestion. Disappointing. We needed more information.*

This is what can happen when you outsource to someone who doesn't know your child or your family. But don't worry, I'm going to teach you how to be your child's best college coach.

Baby steps first. To start, I'll teach you how to be a perfectly adequate college coach so you are comfortable with their ordinary tasks.

Once you understand how to be ordinary, I'll teach you how to be extraordinary. In the second half of this book, I'll show you how you can go beyond OK and become the best possible coach for your child.

.

Chapter 3

What Problem Do You Want to Solve?

What problem are parents trying to solve by hiring a college coach?

I've worked with thousands of homeschool families from around the world. I believe you can group the key issues facing the parents of college-bound teens into three buckets.

1. Parents of teens who are **looking for a specific college**. Often these are elite schools, like Ivies or military academies.

2. Parents who **need their teens to earn scholarships** for college to even be a possibility.

3. Parents who have a student in a unique situation and **need a perfect fit college based on their student's needs or goals**.

Let's look closer at each of these situations so you can discover which one you relate to most.

Problem 1: Your child wants to attend a specific college

Your child's goals can make it a challenge, particularly if your teen wants to attend a specific school such as an Ivy League university, military academy, selective school, or a reach school.

Traci's daughter had her heart set on Pepperdine, an upper echelon school with an amazing beach campus and a California price tag. She needed some help to get admitted to the school and find the scholarships to afford it.

Michele's son wanted to go to West Point – the most elite of the elite schools. It has one of the longest and most arduous application processes. Michelle needed help pulling it all together and making sure nothing was missed.

Problem 2: You need scholarships or college won't be possible

Finances can make college application time stressful, too. This is the most common situation all families face, especially single income families; barring a financial miracle, college won't be practical.

Lin in Washington faced this situation with three high schoolers who had big college dreams. She needed a miracle to help them get through school without a mountain of debt. But Lin was committed and willing to work to help her kids achieve their dreams.

Lori in Idaho felt a mountain of responsibility to help her son make it through college without debt. Like so many others, she was willing to work for the result and her son was on board to do his part.

Problem 3: Your child requires a perfect-fit college

It's also hard to start when you require a perfect fit more than anything, based on your goals for your child in combination with their college and career goals.

This was my concern for Alex, my youngest. He started college at age 16 and had a life-threatening peanut allergy. The college had to be a **perfect** fit – challenging enough for a gifted student, wholesome enough for a young student, and able to keep him alive while eating in the cafeteria for four years. I'm not the only one to face this type of challenge.

Nancy's family also had special circumstances. They were missionaries in the Philippines and their son, Benjamin, wanted to attend a specific school. It was a small Christian school with specific missionary support emphasis and an accredited degree in Industrial Design. Goals don't get much more specific than that.

And then there was Jean, whose daughter was only 16 when she graduated high school. She had specific requirements she wanted to fulfil when she turned to me for help.

So, which situation do you relate to most?

1. **Needing a specific college**

2. **Needing scholarships**

3. **Needing a perfect fit**

Make a mental note of it. We will return to these six families later and reveal how their situations resolved after applying the lessons in this book.

So, let's jump in and learn how you can become your child's best college coach!

Chapter 4

How to Be a Perfectly Adequate College Coach

The first thing a perfectly adequate college coach will do is help the student find a college.

Task 1: Help identify a range of possible colleges

Here's a fun fact – nationwide, only 16 percent of students look for a private college. But when working with a professional college coach, 68 percent look for a private university.

Why the difference? Most parents, working on their own believe that private colleges are too expensive and likely out of their reach. But professional college coaches know that public and private universities often cost about the same after scholarships and grants are applied! In other words, a private or even elite university may be affordable to most parents – you only need to know how the process works.

A perfect fit college means different things to different people and each family prioritizes differently. Here are some of the elements you will naturally consider:

- Admission criteria

- Geographical setting

- Atmosphere

- Academic fit

- Degrees offered

- Size of school

- Public or private

- Religious affiliation

- Cost to attend

- On-time graduation rate

- Average debt upon graduation

- Distance from home

So, how do you find the perfect fit? It starts with planning courses. Eighty-four percent of college coaches advise on academic course selection in high school. I bet 100 percent of you already do this.

Task 2: Help plan junior year

Beyond planning courses, you need to plan junior year carefully, so you can find a college that's a great fit for your student.

Here is the process for junior year:

FALL – Have your child take tests and begin to gather information on colleges. Go to college fairs so you can assess many colleges all at once.

WINTER – Research college statistics, carefully, reading about **only** the colleges your child is interested in.

SPRING – Visit colleges in person, so you know what they are like, beyond the statistics. Then you'll be ready to choose a college your child can apply to and that makes them happy.

Task 3: Whittle down the college list

By the end of junior year, whittle down a list of 4 to 8 colleges where your child will apply. Some consultants suggest 4 to 12 colleges.

What kind of colleges should they apply to? Write this down: *Reach, Fit, Safety, Public, and Private.*

Reach – means your child's SAT or ACT scores are below the college's average, but they meet the requirements.

Fit – means your child's test scores are about the same as the college's average, plus they meet the requirements.

Safety – means your child's test scores are high compared to what that college normally sees. They're more likely to get scholarships, too!

Public – because they have lower tuition but rarely give any meaningful scholarships, you may need to pay much closer to the sticker price.

Private – they have a higher sticker price but are more likely to give big scholarships to qualified students.

Task 4: Help prepare for tests

The next thing a college coach will do is help the student prepare for the SAT or ACT.

1. Advise which test to take and when to take it

2. Advise on test preparation

By the way, only 29 percent of college coaches offer test preparation as part of their services. But you can do this! You have one thing even the best professional coaches don't have – **cookies**!

That's right, cookies are your secret weapon for high school tests! Make a plan for SAT or ACT practice that involves cookies, to help your child earn a higher test score.

Give a timed, SAT sample test in the kitchen. I find that the SAT pairs well with chocolate chip cookies. While your child takes the test, you can bake cookies. Once the test is finished, reward them with cookies and an afternoon free from school. The student will associate the test with pleasure and sweetness, not pain.

Then, give a timed ACT sample test in the kitchen. I find that the ACT pairs well with brownies and chocolate cake –

really, anything chocolate. Once the test is finished, give your child the freshly baked treats.

Compare the sample SAT and ACT scores to see which one is the best fit for your child. Then, have them study regularly for the best test. Three days per week for 20 minutes per day is usually enough.

Pro tip! Focus on improving scores on either the SAT or ACT test, not both. Some college scholarships are automatic, based on SAT or ACT scores.

Choosing the better scoring test could mean a dramatically improved chance of admission, and even better chances for scholarships. It's not uncommon for a child to score in the 50th percentile on one test and the 70th percentile on the other one! Trying both tests at home can make a huge difference to the amount of scholarships awarded.

Next, make a plan for subject tests. It can require some research to help your child choose the right subject tests. There are three kinds:

1. **SAT Subject Test** – high school level and easiest of the three.

2. **AP Tests** – college level, can possibly earn college credit, and can be taken alone or after AP courses.

3. **CLEP Exams** – college level tests. Not all colleges give college credit for CLEPs. But even those that don't grant credit may use CLEP tests to fulfil higher level course prerequisites.

You can find more info on all these tests at CollegeBoard.org.

Task 5: Help brainstorm college application essay topics

Now we get to a place where only the best college coaches live. But it is natural for parents to help brainstorm application essay ideas with their teen because they have lived through the most essay-worthy experiences right alongside their child.

Here are the keys to a perfect application essay

1. Compelling and true story – write that down. This is so the person reading pays attention and remembers your child. Great application essays each paint a different picture of the student.

2. Self-reflective and personal – answers the questions: "Who are you?" and "Are you a good fit?"

3. Technically perfect – answers the questions: "How well can you write?" and "Are you smart enough to succeed in the long run?"

4. Essay topics that are unique to each college – answers the question: "Why should we admit you?" By tailoring essays to each college, your child can demonstrate their interest in that college, which can signal that they will stay for all four years of college.

Pro Tip! In college essays, never repeat anything.

A college may ask for three essays, so make sure the information doesn't overlap. In other words, my son was only allowed to use the word "chess" on **one** essay. A music lover should only write one essay about music – not one on the oboe, one on the orchestra, and one on the piano. You want your student to appear multi-dimensional, rather than just a one-trick pony.

Task 6: Help the student acquire letters of recommendation

Let me explain the four characteristics of a great recommender.

1. They know the student well.

2. They can write well.

3. They can speak to academic preparation.

4. They are not a family member.

Sometimes a college will require the homeschool parent to write the LOR. If so, you must do it. Remember that you are the counselor writing, not the mom or dad. Don't write about anything that happened in your child's life before 9th grade.

The process of acquiring a letter of recommendation is all about the student.

1. The student requests a LOR from a possible recommender.

2. If they say yes, the student provides additional information about themselves to give a fuller picture – perhaps a transcript and activity list.

3. The recommender submits the LOR directly to the college – the student doesn't see it. Scary, right? That's why who you choose is so important.

4. Once you know it's safely at the college, the student sends a thank you note to the recommender.

Task 7: Help the student complete the application

Here's a heads-up for what you will see in the application, so nothing will surprise you.

1. **Fees** – about $50 to $100 per application.

2. **Test scores** – send SAT or ACT scores.

3. **Financial information** – for need-based scholarships.

4. **Recommendation letters** – I already covered these, yay! You know how to take care of these!

5. **Application essays** – Woohoo! You already know how to do these as well!

6. **Application forms** – much like a job application.

7. **Academic records** – including transcript, course descriptions, activity list, reading list, and award list.

8. **Additional paperwork** – colleges may request something unique or unusual.

There are three kinds of application forms.

1. **Common application** – 700 colleges use the common app, so

kids fill out one application for all these colleges.

2. **Coalition application** – about 200 colleges accept the coalition app – this one started because the common app was so expensive and didn't seem to fit many students' needs.

3. **Individual college's own application** – it may be online, downloaded, or on paper. There are so many colleges: Ivy League, low entrance requirement schools, large public universities, smaller or Christian universities. And there are so many types of teens, from public high schools to private schools, Christian schools, and homeschoolers – that using the college's own application is often the easiest route.

Pro Tip! What colleges want is demonstrated interest.

In the application, try to clearly show that your child has demonstrated interest in the college. That's why they should personalize the application essay.

Task 8: Help the student make the final decision.

A good professional college coach may influence the teen to make decisions based on:

- **Prestigious university name or their favorite** – coaches pride themselves on the most prestigious admission. Parents don't have to.

- **Career goals** – the college must offer the degree needed to meet the student's career goals.

- **Financial considerations** – students must be able to afford to go, but professional college coaches may not mind if the parent or student goes into debt. It's not their money, right? Most parents, however, are very concerned about **cost** and **fit**.

There's one big thing you need to remember about making that final decision. Write this down: The National Candidate Reply Date is May 1st so you and your child must decide **before the end of April.** Tell colleges "yes" or "no" when you are sure of your decision. If you delay until after the May 1st deadline, colleges may withdraw their scholarship offers.

OK, we have talked through the eight things a professional college coach does: help identify colleges, plan junior year, whittle down, prepare for tests, brainstorm application essay topics, get recommendations, complete the application, and make the final decision.

Now let's talk about how they do it.

Task 9: Guide the process as a project manager.

What is a project manager? My husband was a project manager at Boeing. He didn't make the airplanes; he made sure the airplanes were made correctly and on time. You are the project manager - not the builder or the doer. That's what you have been doing as a homeschool parent all along, right?

The project manager:

- Makes the plans

- Delegates the tasks

- Oversees the project

- Ensures quality

You are ultimately responsible that the work gets done properly and on time.

Pro Tip! Begin applications on the first day of 12th grade.

Homeschoolers can incorporate the work of applying to college right into your normal school day and it will be much easier for everyone.

Chapter 5

How to be the Best College Coach

You've learned how to be a perfectly adequate college coach; you've gone through each task a normal college coach would perform. And I've told you what to do for each of those tasks. But that's not all. You are here to learn how to be your child's **best** college coach. In this chapter, I explain what will make you stand out, head and shoulders above any professional college coaches you could choose.

Task 1: Meet with your student.

Sounds ridiculous, but only six percent of college coaches meet their students in person. The vast majority meet by phone or online. How many times have you met your student in person? Today, for example . . . at breakfast?

Think for a moment about the information only you know. In your notebook, write down:

- Motivation

- Compliance

- Follow-through

- Genuine interests

- Real financial situation

- Family values

- Spiritual goals

- Five-year plan for your family

Perhaps you don't want to tell a stranger why you make certain choices about college. After all, some colleges allow behavior that is legal but not edifying for your child. Perhaps this total stranger, the college coach, wants your child to be more assimilated into a society that shares their values but not your values.

Be glad you can guide your child as their best college coach. And think about your five-year plan for your family. Perhaps you are prioritizing a happy, healthy, close, extended family with your grown adult child more than a prestigious degree at a far-away college.

Task 2: Use information about your unique situation.

Here's an interesting statistic. Twenty percent of students choose an out-of-state college. But 69 percent of professionally coached students choose an out-of-state college. There's nothing wrong with going out of state for college but I feel more comfortable if the parent is guiding that choice, not a stranger.

In your notebook, write down some examples in your family that make your situation unique.

You have unique goals - faith-based colleges, Ivy league dreams, military academics, or a geographical location closer to home.

You have unique requirements - a struggling learner, an NCAA athlete, you live overseas, have a National Merit Scholar, or your child wants to take a gap year.

Every family is unique. As I mentioned before, I have a son with a life-threatening peanut allergy. We had to find a college that could fit **and** keep him alive for four whole years. In addition, he was ready and eager to start his college studies at age 16, so the college needed to be wholesome enough to for a younger student. Finding a suitable college was a challenge!

Task 3: Use information learned from homeschooling.

In your notebook, write down some examples. Think about all the skills you have learned while you have been homeschooling! Eighteen percent of college coaches include assistance with academic tutoring. And to think, 100 percent of homeschool parents are already doing this! You know how to facilitate learning, you know how to encourage active participation, and you know how to motivate your student to follow through. Provide academic tutoring? Yes, as you have always done.

And finally, you have learned the importance of why you invest in education. You have spent money on curriculum, experiences, and educational opportunities the whole time you have been homeschooling. You know that investing in education is important and has long term benefits, far beyond measure.

Pro Tip! You can replace normal homeschool work with test prep and applications.

You already know how to mix and match curriculum, right? Consider this senior year work as part of your normal homeschool. Only 29 percent of college coaches offer test preparation as part of their services but you can easily include this as part of your normal school work each day. They do this in elite college prep high schools, and you can do it too!

Task 4: Help your student earn scholarships.

The fourth way you are awesome is that you can help your student earn scholarships. Only 43 percent of professional college coaches offer financial aid information – isn't that surprising? You would think this would be fundamental. So, write down "Invest in education." You've done so all these years and it continues to be a good investment. You may want to look up Proverbs 3:13-14 for some added encouragement.

So, invest in wisdom! But that doesn't mean go into debt. College is not usually cost-free but college can be debt-free and homeschoolers can earn scholarships. Let me explain.

There are three kinds of scholarships

1. Need-based scholarships, based on your family finances as stated on your IRS forms.

2. Merit scholarships awarded by each specific college based on the *awesomeness* of your child.

3. Private scholarships are provided by companies, not colleges, so you need to apply separately from the college application.

This next pro tip is critical!

Pro Tip! All scholarships are first-come, first-served. Don't merely get it in before the deadline – get it in well before the deadline.

Task 5: Help the student learn life skills.

Here's something that no professional college coach will do – prepare teens for independent living by teaching the most important skills.

Here are the four steps to teaching these skills:

1. Discuss what to do

2. Demonstrate what to do

3. Practice what to do

4. Perfect the most important life skills

This is important because someday your child will live on their own. They will sink or swim based on the skills you have given them and their ability to adapt as an adult. They will leave home with or without these skills, so try to cover them over the four years of high school so they can survive and thrive.

Task 6: Help the student find career guidance.

Find the calling that's right for them. Is that college, entrepreneurship, or trade school? If you spend $5000 on a college coach and then your child decides not to go to college, that money is wasted! By being your child's college coach, you can guide them toward college but not be stressed or frustrated about them choosing trade school. This allows more flexibility. Give your child the skills they need for **both** college and career success and make sure they can maintain a resumé.

Pro Tip! Delight directed learning is career guidance – it can help them shape and mold

their interests, calling, and passions. As a bonus, it makes homeschooling more fun for the child and easier on parents.

Task 7: Help the student prepare for college success.

Incidentally, this isn't covered by a professional college coach. It's not enough to get there, you want your child to thrive! Spend some time and effort giving advice before they head off. Explain how to study at college and teach them how to write for college. And most importantly for Christians, explain the keys to retaining their faith while in college. In fact, I think it's time for another pro tip for families of faith!

Pro Tip! Your goal is for your child to attend church within the first three weeks on campus.

Some research suggests that teens who attend a church or faith event within the first three weeks of college are more likely to retain their faith. You need to locate a good church and church group while visiting colleges. This is not something you can delegate to a professional coach.

Task 8: Help the student successfully enter adulthood.

How do you do so? **Encourage independence**. Keep your five-year plan in mind. In five years, you want to have a happy, healthy, and close extended family. When conflict occurs during college, step in only when your child is engaging in something *life-threateningly* stupid (like drugs) *or life-alteringly* stupid (like criminal behavior). As much as possible, allow natural consequences, which is what adults use to make good decisions. They don't use nagging or advice, they use the experience of natural consequences.

Here's another job a great college coach must do. **You must help the student's parent cope with the empty nest.**

Yes, that's you, the parent! You need to help yourself. Plan for the end of homeschooling. Yes, you get tired and need to stop each day – that's ok! Do your best, as you are able. Then you can live life after homeschooling with no regrets, knowing you gave it your all.

Chapter 6

Four College Coaching Options

Whether you realize it or not, there will be some college coaching required if your child is going to college. The key is to know what the options are, so you can choose what is right for your family.

Option 1: The Laissez Faire Method

Giving your child the responsibility to get into college often becomes the default position for parents who are simply not paying attention. Frankly, I see this a lot in public school parents. It can mean flailing, where your method is best described as sink-or-swim or point-

and-pray. You are letting the teen figure it out on their own.

I've had a parent say to me, "I worked my way through college with grants and student loans. Why shouldn't my teen do the same?" This sounds nice, until you realize that your *strategy* may mean your child leaves college saddled with thousands of dollars, if not hundreds of thousands, in student debt.

This is what happened to my niece. Over a decade later, she is still paying back student loans.

This approach can sound awesome because it's easy on Mom and Dad, but the costs of a single teen failure anywhere along the process can be huge. One missed deadline or misguided decision can cost $10,000 or more.

My accountant used this approach and his daughter missed **one** deadline! She qualified for a-full tuition scholarship but because she missed the deadline, she had to pay full price! Yikes!

Remember the job of the project manager? If a teenager is the project manager, you can't ensure quality. With the laissez-faire method, a 17-year-old has ultimate authority over your college budget. Scary!

Option 2: The Do-it-Yourself Alternative

This is a less expensive option but it can be stressful. You can opt to find no-cost or low-cost training to guide you. Courses are all over the internet but, like all online advice, it may be incomplete, unproven, or flat out wrong. For example, I saw one course that offered 6 hours of online training with 10 worksheets – the focus was **only** Ivy league schools and nothing homeschool focused, for $295.

Alternatively, you can reinvent the wheel and go-it-alone. In addition to learning all the tricks of the trade yourself, you have to be on top of guiding your student so they don't miss anything. One slip can be very expensive. Also, do you have all the extra hours you'll need for this alternative?

Homeschool parents have many other responsibilities – other children, a home to care for, meals to manage, a household to run. We don't do this in a vacuum. And have you noticed your family wants dinner **every night?**

Option 3: Outsourcing a College Coach

Many public and private school parents with the means decide to hire a college coach because their high school guidance counselor isn't helping. Before we talk about money, let's look at the big picture. Do you know the person who is **most** influential to launch success? It isn't you and it isn't a college coach . . . it is your student.

While spending thousands may motivate you to stay on track with tasks, **it may not motivate your student.** And if your teen doesn't do their part, all that money you spend on a college coach will be wasted. You may not experience the success you expect based on the cost you paid.

As I mentioned, the average cost of a college coach in the U.S. is $4000 to $6000. Some are **much** more – $100,000 to $200,000. You might be wondering if there are any professional college coaches who work specifically with homeschoolers. Yes! They should be more affordable, right?

No! One college coach works specifically with homeschoolers aiming for Ivy schools. The price is $5750 for one year of help. Even so, you could end up paying at or near full-price for college. Or your student could end up at a college that doesn't fit – one that might ruin the young adult, their faith, their potential, and their future career.

So, what does the average person do? Lacking this sort of money, most public and private school parents rely on their school's guidance counselor. (If you homeschool, that's you!)

Again, the problem for public school parents is that the average high school guidance counselor has 478 students to guide, so their time and help is limited.

The cost isn't only monetary. Don't forget the high cost of fear. An article in USA today says there is one reason people hire professional college coaches – fear.

High school students and their parents have become so panicked with the mystique surrounding today's college admissions process that they are clamoring to find help to better their odds in the college admissions game. That, along with the lack of quality admission counseling in the high schools, has been a boon for independent education consultants.

~ "Is hiring a college planner worth it?" - USA Today Nov. 15, 2014

Fear has amazing power and can cause some really regrettable decisions. There are several reasons for this.

- **Fear immobilizes** – it keeps you from taking action.

- **Fear makes you passive** – you become more willing to blindly accept advice from people who don't know your family.

- **Fear clouds your judgement** – you stop looking at things objectively.

- **Fear removes your power** – delegating your kids future to anyone removes your power; you become a victim of the system instead of an overcomer. But you aren't a victim!

You are strong – you are a parent! Hear us roar, right?

Option 4: Embrace Your Role as the Best College Coach

Parents are different. You know your child! You love the high school student you are guiding! You didn't need professional training in *classroom management* to successfully teach your teen. And you don't need professional college coaching either, because you don't need to know everything for everyone – you simply need to know your child.

You can become the BEST college coach for your child. You can do it yourself . . . except for a few things. Let's talk about what's missing

1. You are missing some knowledge. Most parents don't live, breathe, and sleep college admission, so your understanding of the ever-changing admission process might be a bit lacking. You would love to have the time to research all that is needed to successfully guide your student, but other things keep getting in the way, such as feeding kids and teaching them. But what you do know is your child. You don't have to do any research on your child, which is a huge benefit.

2. You need some encouragement. Launching your child, even in the best circumstances can be overwhelming and emotional. At times, you will feel discouraged, depressed, and unappreciated. You want the best for your child – for them to graduate without debt and be happy in future.

3. You are missing accountability. We all know that the urgent (such as getting dinner on the table and getting to practices on time) always seems to take precedence over the important (application essays, deadlines, and test prep). You need some accountability to keep on task.

4. You're missing an investment!

You need to invest in education – an emotional and monetary investment. Each college coaching option has a cost and I think we can agree it is crazy expensive to hire a professional coach.

Most homeschool families are single income and often don't have a spare $4000 lying around the house. Heck, most families where both parents work don't have that kind of spare change. That's why they are both working, right?

Often, homeschoolers are very aware of the burden of debt and are willing to invest in resources that will help them avoid the burden of debt. This makes the investment in education even more important.

As the number of homeschoolers increase and larger numbers of parents gear up to graduate their children, I have felt a growing burden to help families toward their end game - the latter half of their high school career – the college and career launch.

I developed the **College Launch Solution** to provide in-depth training for parents who want to be their child's best college coach. I want to save parents the exorbitant expense of hiring a professional coach, as well as save them from the anxiety and fear that comes with the *laissez faire method* or going it alone. I want to provide enough training, encouragement, and accountability to make the task reasonable, but not impossible.

If you are curious about whether the College Launch Solution will work for you, I encourage you to go to www.CollegeLaunchSolution.com to learn more.

For more in-depth information, this link will tell you what's inside this comprehensive on-line resource: https://goo.gl/1uFFXY

Finally, if you would prefer to simply poke around the product itself, you can go to this link: https://goo.gl/4QZ8AW

There, you can explore all the product modules, but the links won't be live until you purchase.

Chapter 7

My Journey Through College and Launch

Can you believe you have a child almost old enough to leave home? Scary, right? How did your baby grow up so fast?

In the next chapter, I'll share the heartfelt survey responses I received when I asked parents to describe their journey toward homeschool graduation and launch.

But to start, I want to share a little bit about my own journey and struggles, so you know that I've been where you are and lived to tell the tale. It will be interesting to see what sounds familiar to you.

When I was homeschooling, I noticed that once we got into the upper grades, so many faithful homeschool families seemed to give up and put their kids into public or private school. Frankly, I didn't understand why. Homeschooling for us had been so much fun and successful in the early days that I was mystified by why someone would ever choose to walk away from it.

Gradually, though, as they dropped out, I started to feel anxiety and doubt. What about college, career, or scholarships? And what about the teaching physics and the ever-present "What about socialization?"

Thankfully, my best friend was a life-long homeschooler, ready with encouragement. Her kids were normal nerdy boys about my own kids' age, so we had a lot in common. The friendship was fun, easy, and always encouraging. I've done a lot of thinking about why Debbie made such a positive impact on our homeschooling career. I came up with three big reasons.

1. She was real. Debbie wasn't perfect and her homeschool certainly wasn't perfect. She didn't intimidate me like some of my Ivy bound homeschool friends in my old neighborhood. Her kids weren't perfect. They were normal. All of them were bright but had their share of learning challenges. I was never blown away by negative comparisons with her children that made me feel inadequate

2. She took time for me. My perpetual questions were never a bother. Debbie had learned enough in her homeschooling years to help me avoid some of the hidden traps. She offered quiet encouragement and help when I had trouble figuring something out.

3. She let me learn on my own. Debbie wasn't pushy about how things had to be done. She offered suggestions and things to try but never made me feel bad if something that worked for her didn't work for me.

When I started The HomeScholar, one of my unspoken goals was to be a *Debbie* for other homeschoolers and try to embody these helpful characteristics for others. So, for over 10 years now, I have been able to personally partner with over 5000 homeschool families, coming alongside each of them to teach solutions for different homeschool high school issues.

In addition, I have provided free resources to the broader homeschool community, from a monthly newsletter, free online workshops, and regular blog posts, to social media where I have reached hundreds of thousands of families.

My passion for homeschooling high school has led me to author 35 books (and counting) on the topic and create a vast set of free resources that have been shared with tens of thousands of families. I count it all joy as it validates that my current calling has been from the Lord and He has made it so fruitful.

Now, let's look at the questions and challenges of regular families I have helped in their quest to successfully launch their children from homeschool into a bright future.

Chapter 8

The HomeScholar Answers Your Questions about College and Launch

This is the hardest chapter to write, because it's not a concrete set of solutions. But I also think this chapter is going to be the most relatable because these struggles will sound familiar to most of you. As always, I promise not to leave you in despair. (Remember, I'm the homeschool consultant who **won't** make you cry.) I will offer you hope and a clear path toward launch success.

The whole college and launch appears to be the leading cause for an untold number of panicky days and sleepless nights. So, I want to take a moment to share a few of these survey responses I received from families around the world who are all experiencing some seriously strong emotions about the launch situations they are facing.

I seemed to get three kinds of comments from my survey. First, the *Fears and Tears* – panicky parents having a serious meltdown. Second, the *Cheers* – those who are so happy about the process and where they are within it. And third, what I call *Wet-Behind-the-Ears* – the newbies, like a toddler starting to walk – neither scared nor celebrating, simply struggling to figure things out.

Fears and Tears

Question: *How do I go through this process without stressing my student out (and myself as well)? Where do I get info about scholarships (besides those huge books in the library)?*

Answer: I love this question because it's so important to stay calm during high school. You are trying to develop a warm, loving family relationship for the future, so when your child is grown they don't resent you or resent homeschooling. And yes, avoiding major stress is a great idea! Here's the answer – write this down. **The key is to swap one kind of schoolwork for another kind of schoolwork.**

Instead of adding test prep **and** scholarship writing, replace schoolwork with the new work. It's a trade. Instead of vocabulary workbooks, consider the test prep book your child's vocabulary workbook. Instead of purchasing an English program for the year, assign your child real writing practice daily, by writing application essays and scholarship essays.

Question: *My biggest concern is how to prep my kids for the onslaught of anti-Christian worldview attacks in* *every area of campus life . . . inside the classroom and out (residence halls and general school policies).*

Answer: I know how you feel – I looked out at the world, considered the present evil age, and wondered what to do. It's scary! You know, in the Old Testament, the Jews were scared to go into the promised land because of the big, scary people they saw. God doesn't want us to be afraid – he wants faith in action.

Let me give you two scriptures. Write these down: Mark 16:15 says, "Go into all the world and preach the good news to all creation." And 1 Corinthians 13:11 says, "When I was a child, I spoke like a child, I thought like a child, I reasoned like a child. When I became a man, I gave up childish ways."

Let's consider this. As Christians, we are called to go into **all** the world – no exceptions. And you see in scripture how mature adults do go into the whole world – even in places rough around the edges, anti-Christian, and spiritually bankrupt.

At some point, we must let our children engage the fallen world so they can change the culture. If your child's plan includes college, search for the best fit of course! At the same time, don't let them become immobilized.

Let me put it another way – in the Bible, Paul mixed it up with secular people noted for their immorality in that day. He was a tent-maker, so I'm sure they were rough around the edges. It was like the secular colleges of that time.

He also worked with the Sadducees and Pharisees, the "Christian college crowd" of the time. He could do this because he was an adult, grounded in the Word, working in a team. Instead of preventing them from making adult decisions and leading an adult life, help your child find a team to walk alongside – a cohort to go with your child through that experience, such as a campus ministry group. Don't let those fears prevent you from launching your adult. You see, we **homeschool** children, but we **launch** adults into the world.

Question: *We hired a college coach, I feel she was totally off the mark with her suggestion. Disappointing. We needed more information.*

Answer: Yes! This is the problem with college coaches! They don't know the full story of who your child is and what you as the parent want for them! What you need from a college coach is someone who truly knows your child, to help guide them to the best fit.

I believe that a hired college coach will never be as good as a parent coach because you know your child best. It's much more effective to have the parent do limited research on colleges their child is interested in, going through a clearly explained process to find those colleges, and then focusing on in-depth research of a few.

With a coach, your child is only guided to colleges the coach knows best, with no guarantee they are a good fit. A college coach will try to get your child into the best possible college – often without understanding your financial situation or family values. These are just a few reasons why the best college coach is you!

Question: *Know that not everyone is fortunate enough to afford college. Be real about having to work while going to college.*

Answer: I think it's a common myth that college is unaffordable. But do consider that it **always** costs money to launch a child. Think about it. They need to get started in housing and transportation, right? And with careful planning, you can arrange college admission for a college that you (and they) can afford. It's probably not going to be free, but it can be affordable.

Sometimes affordable does mean that the child works while going to college. Statistically, though, kids working through college do great! Because they need to be more organized to get it all done, and because they are more personally invested financially, they tend to do better in college. They are motivated to get done on time and more eager to find a well-paying job at the end. Plus, they have a great resume four years later with both college **and** work on their resume!

Question: *I have already had two kids go through the process and I am on my third child (and last) however, every child is different. So, we will see how this will go for us. Conditions are always changing as far as what's required and needed at colleges now-a-*

-days. It's good to keep up with the current information and knowhow.

Answer: Yes, indeed! The conditions are always changing and what colleges want changes from year-to-year. What your child wants may change year-to-year as well. That's why it's important to be prepared for everything with your college prep plan – and remain flexible though junior and senior year. This is also why a parent can be their child's best college coach. As each child matures, you don't need to stay on top of all colleges across the U.S. – you only need to do current research on colleges your child is interested in. I would love to help you work in the "here and now" with steps that are clearly laid out in the College Launch Solution.

Cheers

It's not all bad news and concerns – other parents like you have experienced great encouragement and success!

Question: *Each aspect of college and launch have been a concern at different points in the process. But you, Lee, made things so much easier with your amazing guidance and instruction – you demystified the application process for us. My son was accepted into all the colleges he applied to, so now we're at the point of making the final decision, which is hard in its own way, even though it's a joyful, happy, positive thing! We appreciate even the most basic of information – tips and pointers that may seem obvious, but we might have overlooked. So, yes, please I'm eager for more of the practical succeeding in college guidance! Thank you!*

Answer: I loved reading this comment because I thought it would be encouraging! You see how she feels things weren't so bad. As she went through the process with me, the process was made easier and demystified. And now, praise the Lord, she is facing final decisions and is joyful!

This mom is now facing the "letting go" stage, which can be so emotional! And in those final months before your child leaves home, it's good to focus on how to succeed in college – teaching them life skills, study skills – concrete things like how to talk to a professor, and what a syllabus is and why it's important.

Being eager for guidance is a clear sign of success. Write this down: A parent who is eager to learn is a parent who will experience success in the college launch.

Question: *Lee, if you were to do college coaching, we would seriously consider it. There are too many hacks out there, misguiding people with their finances and couldn't advise on a well-written essay if it hit them in the face. Because it is hard to know who is worth $4000, we are very hesitant to spend it. We have looked at many. You make it* *sound so simple and these other people/companies make it sound so hard. Does the college game really require a college coach to do it well or only if the kid is going after upper echelon schools?*

Answer: Wow, what a blessing to read that note! Yes, when I was homeschooling, I could never have afforded $4000 for a college coach. I know one college coach who specializes in homeschoolers who want to attend Ivy league schools, and he charges up to $9500 for help! It may be helpful, but at the same time, wow! Who can afford that? And what if you find out that they aren't as like-minded as you had hoped?

I don't think college coaches are bad people – they do a lot of great work! But here's the thing – we are parents who have been homeschooling. We have learned to become teachers for our children. Not a teacher for 30 children this year and another 30 next year. No, you focus on only your child.

And you can learn to become a guidance counselor and plan classes and tests for your child. Not a guidance counselor for 478 kids – only your child. And just like we learned to teach reading and writing, we can also learn how to be college coaches. Not for all kids and all universities. We only need to guide **our** child, and the few universities they find interesting.

Even in the upper echelon colleges of Harvard and West Point, homeschoolers have been admitted without using a professional college coach. Sometimes I think they simply find us refreshing, you know? Something new?

I have read that at elite schools, the admission rate for homeschoolers is higher than the admission rate for public/private schooled kids. I recently celebrated with one member whose son will be going to West Point and two years ago, a member's daughter entered!

So yes, it's possible for parents to manage the process since they know their child, love their child, and know what's important to them and their child. Write this down: You only need to guide your child, even if they're going for upper echelon colleges.

Question: *I enjoyed and used your resources to help my oldest daughter get accepted with scholarships into every college or university she applied to. She decided she didn't want to attend any of them and opted to complete a program at our local community college.*

Answer: Yay, college admission and scholarships! She was prepared with maximum flexibility, right? At the end of senior year, she was given a choice of university, community college, and employment. What an amazing thing, to be offered that much flexibility – to have three great options to choose from!

This is why you want to be prepared for anything. This young lady was planning on a four-year college, and ultimately chose another route. I'm so glad they didn't pay $4000 for a college coach. I'm glad this parent was the best college coach for her child, using resources I provided.

They had the flexibility without the pressure to attend the most prestigious option to get "their money's worth." Be prepared for anything and present your own child with some great options, too. And you want to be in a place to make that decision without financial pressure. Again, **flexibility** is the key ingredient here.

Question: *Your coaching is so helpful. I get tiny bits of information that I can process without being overwhelmed. I don't know what I don't know . . . so I* *also get answers to questions that I hadn't even considered asking!*

Answer: I know it can be overwhelming sometimes. That's why the College Launch Solution offers a group coaching option. When I give moms a huge amount of information, some parents thrive, but others get overwhelmed and can't see the forest for the trees. What I've done is prepared a monthly email for everyone who is a group coaching member. You'll get an assignment for each month based on your child's age. One assignment per month, whew! Quite a relief, right? Well, I've also included a tip for teens each month – and for those who are financially strapped, a money-saving tip you can use as well. I tried to break it down into tiny bits of information.

Listen, even with a monthly email, I know some parents will still feel overwhelmed and need to talk and have someone listen and help them assess the issues. That's why the College Launch Solution also offers a private coaching option, so you can I can talk together, sharing coffee over the phone for 20 minutes each week. When you are confused, this can be a Godsend, you know? And that's what the private coaching option is for – in case you might need some personal encouragement that can't come through a group setting.

Question: *We are currently getting ready to launch our youngest into college. We have homeschooled both of our sons from the start of schooling. Our oldest was accepted to 25 colleges and universities. He is now doing well in his junior year of college with tremendous scholarships. Our youngest has been accepted to 24 colleges and universities and will soon need to make a decision on which one he will attend. He also has tremendous scholarship opportunities! Thank you so much for your many years of wisdom and* *encouragement!! I often point people to your website, Facebook page, and materials!!*

Answer: I think it's so important for us all to look past the here and now, and see that homeschoolers do achieve college admission, and they do get tremendous scholarships. I want to spend a moment to think about how homeschoolers thrive – as this mom said her child is doing well as a college junior. Think about this – I can't tell you how many parents have written to me, shocked that their child got such good grades in college. Why are they shocked? Because in college they are being compared to others who have not been homeschooled, often for the first time.

As a homeschooler, you generally try to get your child to learn something before moving on. That's called *mastery*. You want them to both know and understand. You watch them do the work. Those are the practices that create great college students. Being a homeschooler is great preparation for life after launch. It gives them the work ethic, study ethic, and the expectation of learning independently. I guess I want to say, "Go team go! Yay homeschoolers!"

Wet Behind the Ears

Question: *Guiding the clueless parents, make sure there are no gaps in the process. We have big fear that we are doing something in high school (or not doing) that will hurt our child's chances of being accepted at an ideal university that seems to be best suited for our child.*

Answer: Such a heart-felt response. I can feel the anxiety. I totally understand! Part of being the high school guidance counselor is making sure your child has the classes they need and the tests they need, and identifying any gaps. Remember that not all gaps are important. Sometimes parents think they missed a subject, such as state history, and later realize it wasn't required in their state. Other times, a parent can quickly fill a gap when necessary.

I'll tell you a little story about a huge gap in my own homeschool. I forgot to teach one child economics. Since the other child worked on economics all day for fun for years, it totally slipped my mind that his brother hadn't taken any economics! But I was able to quickly fill that gap. So here is what you need to write down: Get information so you can find the gaps that are natural for everyone. Then locate a resource to quickly fill the gap without panicking because again, these are natural for everyone. Identify and fill gaps quickly.

Question: *I need a timeline for all four years of high school on what we should be preparing to do next for college admission, scholarships, and getting all* *our information ready for the process. I have done this twice, but it is always helpful to have a checklist for the next three.*

Answer: I understand needing a timeline. In my newsletter, I always include calendar reminders for each year of high school. In my membership plans, I include a college prep calendar. I also have application tracking checklists and checklists for comparing college offers.

You know what I've found out? A timeline, calendar, and checklist aren't enough for the average homeschool parent. Like having food in the refrigerator isn't enough – you still need to cook the food for dinner, right? And with this timeline and college admission and scholarships, you need to do the work and that requires motivation. Write that down: Get the motivation to do the work.

That's why the College Launch Solution includes the group coaching option. Yes, you will get that timeline, but you'll also get an email reminder each month, to keep you on track. Plus, you'll get access to an exclusive group of members you can chat with, so you can be in a group of like-minded parents talking about topics such as the SAT or application essays. I know you need a timeline but each child is so unique. You can be the best college counselor and get the information that you need, when you need it.

Question: *I think instead of helping me, you should be speaking to my kids. You have sage advice. They might listen to you when they won't listen to me.*

Answer: Oh boy, do I hear you! Because you're right, sometimes teens will listen to an authority when they don't listen to a parent who says the exact same thing. I used to tell my ploddingly-careful son not to take so much time on his work. "Stop after an hour," I said! "When you sit there for more than an hour you are less productive." He didn't believe me.

Flash forward. Now he has his master's degree, and studies psychology for fun. He came to me with a startling revelation the other day. "Look mom," he says, "you have to tell this to homeschoolers." Did you know that humans learn best when they concentrate for an hour or less, and get less productive after that? You should tell homeschoolers to move at least every hour and not try to push through a lesson when it takes longer than that." So yeah . . . my own child. Didn't. Listen.

This is why the College Launch Solution includes a teen track, four-hour workshop, so I can say what the teens need to know, directly from me (the "expert-who-is-not-mom") to the young adult who needs the information. Sure, they can join you for the detailed one-hour class on every aspect as well, and I hope they do! But the four-hour workshop should give them enough information to do a great job. So, write this down: Teens need to think about what comes after high school and how to succeed in college.

Question: *We're homeschooling our first high schooler and she has two sisters right behind her. While she does have some serious interest in pursuing a career in the culinary field, she's still unsure about what she'd like to "be when she grows up." I do not have a college education and became a full time SAHM mom when I was in my 20s. My husband did not attend college, but served in the army for four years and has since led a professional career in the transportation industry for 20+ years without a degree.*

We aren't sure how to help direct our daughter's goals or if that is even possible at her age to have a definite career/life plan. We would appreciate information and insight on how best to educate, guide, and graduate a homeschooler that may not have a definite major or career in mind. Thank you

Answer: I totally understand – not all parents are familiar with the college application process! Many haven't gone through the process of applying themselves and if they have, they find the process has changed so dramatically that they don't even recognize the steps anymore. Others are from other countries, unfamiliar with the U.S. system of education and college applications.

That's why I try so hard to make it easy for parents. When I explain that sophomore means 10th grader, and junior means 11th grader, I'm not trying to talk down to anyone, I promise! It's because some parents haven't learned things yet that other parents find elementary.

I work hard to provide step-by-step simple instructions for parents with normal teens – and to be clear, normal teens are frequently unsure about what they want to do! Like you, I was a stay-at-home mom in a single income family. Finding scholarships was the only way we could afford college.

My suggestion to best guide your daughter is to be ready for anything – college or career. If she gets married early, great! She is better prepared to make up her mind about what she wants to do. If she doesn't get married quickly, great! Like me, she can use her degree to serve others until her mission in life changes.

Many women have multiple careers over their lifetime, right? I was a nurse, then a mom, then a homeschooler, and now a small business owner. Making one decision right now doesn't mean she won't change her mind multiple times. And the summary of all her experiences will be used to better our society and the culture in the long run.

Question: *I need successful options for types of curriculum/courses accepted by colleges. I have a child who is dyslexic and we need to think outside the box on the courses he takes but would still like to know how colleges might view these types of courses.*

Answer: I've tried hard to include information to help you be a college coach in a variety of different scenarios. You see, some parents are gearing up for the military, some are missionaries overseas, some have struggling learners or children with disabilities, and some are considering an NCAA sport in college.

Each of these scenarios has a unique set of issues. How could a college coach know them all? They can't, and you don't need to know them all, either. You only need to know what unique issues your child faces, and then find out where to get the answers.

Often, a starting piece of information and a listening ear to help you brainstorm ideas is all you need. It helps to have a fellow homeschooler who can help you take these strange and new pieces of information and apply them to your normal and natural homeschool, to avoid becoming overwhelmed. For example, if you have carefully guided your child to avoid labeling, how do you suddenly do a 180 and decide to accept a label to access the services that will benefit your child?

Sometimes the best way is to talk about it with another homeschool parent – someone who understands both labeling and the importance of finding resources, so you can weigh the pros and cons with an understanding friend.

Question: *The public school system doesn't inform or prepare you, the parent, for what tests should be done, when, or even how to prepare your child for going to college. I've learned more from the homeschool community than I would have ever learned from public schools – even though I seem to be arriving into homeschooling very late in the game. I need to catch up to speed fast. So far, it's a lot of trial and error. Where do I start, what's a priority, and how do I catch up and learn without wasting too much time? It is overwhelming.*

Answer: Oh boy, isn't that the truth? It's tempting to think that in a public school this stuff would be handled for you – but it's **not**. A school may have 500 students per guidance counselor – they seriously only have time to handle the kids who are in big trouble, not track down each child for tests or inform parents of details.

That's why parents are so much better at being the guidance counselor! You may have many kids, but not 500, that's for sure! It's easier for you to keep on track, even during your full-time job of homeschooling, than it is for a guidance counselor to keep on track because they also have a more than full-time job handling a boatload of students!

Frankly, it's the same issue with college counselors – they have so many colleges, career choices, and kids to keep track of . . . it's easier for a parent to guide their small cohort of high schoolers whom they love and want the best for. Homeschool parents often feel the need to catch up and learn without wasting time, so you can be the best guide for college. You can do it! And I'm here to help!

Question: *I am taking a moment to thank you for the seminars you have provided over the years – they have helped us launch our first child into* *college. After a wonderful choice for academics and athletics, he transferred the next year because he saw that worldview and connections with like-minded people made more sense than the constant barrage of negativity toward other opinions/unwillingness to discuss. Though he still has these original goals, he has never felt held back by homeschooling and sees that it makes the difference in his life and, he hopes, in others. Some of that comes from the confidence of parenting through homeschooling high school and you have provided assistance in that area! Thank you.*

Answer: Such a sweet note! When I was homeschooling, I loved hearing *war stories* from those who have taken the plunge into homeschooling high school and saw it through until success.

Conclusion

I hope these stories have been encouraging to you as you face your child's launch into adulthood. We've been over quite a few comments from other real parents like you. I hope these genuine, heart-felt survey responses will comfort you, so you know you are **not** alone in your insecurities.

My goal for this book is to provide you with something tangible as you come face-to-face with your child's college launch. As I have trained thousands of parents on how to be the best possible guidance counselor for their kids, I hope you will trust me to teach you how to be your child's best possible college coach.

If you are ready to take on this role, here is a $75 off promo code you can use for your purchase of the College Launch Solution.

www.CollegeLaunchSolution.com
use promo code **cls75**

I am very excited to meet you, get to know your story, and help you along the road. The best part, however, by far, will be celebrating with you when your child has been launched successfully into adult life. The joy, pride, and relief you will feel over this "job well done" is something you will carry with you for the rest of your life.

Afterword

Who is Lee Binz and What Can She Do for Me?

Number one best-selling homeschool author, Lee Binz, is The HomeScholar. Her mission is "helping parents homeschool high school." Lee and her husband, Matt, homeschooled their two boys, Kevin and Alex, from elementary through high school.

Upon graduation, both boys received four-year, full tuition scholarships from their first-choice university. This enables Lee to pursue her dream job – helping parents homeschool their children through high school.

On The HomeScholar website, you will find great products for creating homeschool transcripts and comprehensive records to help you amaze and impress colleges.

Find out why Andrew Pudewa, Founder of the Institute for Excellence in Writing says, "Lee Binz knows how to navigate this often confusing and frustrating labyrinth better than anyone."

You can find Lee online at:

www.HomeHighSchoolHelp.com

If this book has been helpful, could you please take a minute to write us a quick review on Amazon?

Thank you!

Testimonials

Our whole family is gaining the confidence to launch our children

The College Launch Solution is a great resource!!! It is absolutely what I was hoping for! I felt like we had just an OK handle on all that we needed to do to help our children graduate and be ready for college. **But now, I KNOW we can do it with your help!!**

I've already worked my way through the first three modules! I have a rising senior and want to use this summer to glean all I can from it. I love the fact that I do have access for three years, though, because I also have a rising sophomore, so I know I will keep coming back to it!

I have always enjoyed your webinars, as each one is full of such helpful information. They have given me so much confidence in knowing I COULD homeschool high school. Now, with the College Launch Solution, I feel our whole family is gaining the confidence to launch our children into college and beyond.

My daughter had a mini freak out just a couple of weeks before the College Launch Solution came out as she was looking ahead to her senior year. All of it was a bit overwhelming for her. After she attended the College Admission Seminar for Teens, she was so much more calm and confident. She said, "Mom, it's just step-by-step. I thought I had to do it all in the first month of next year! But now I know I can just take it one thing at a time."

My favorite quote from you is, "Keep your five- year plan in mind, to have a happy, healthy, close extended family." I found myself getting bogged down and only thinking about how to get through her senior year and helping her get into college. This quote jolted me into a major perspective shift!! It helped me see (and quite frankly, remember) that college is not life! It is just one of the steps leading to success as an adult.

I have also really loved the "extras" you include. Not the major bonuses, although those are terrific! But I'm talking about things like all the handouts with nice, neat outlines, the year-by-year prep plans, the Guide to College Costs, and the College Application Tracker. **Real practical stuff that helps keep me organized!!!** I am a very organized person by nature, and before the College Launch Solution, I kept searching for things like this. I found a few items, but having it all in one place really speaks deeply to my organizer's heart!!! THANK YOU!!!

~ Johanna in Nebraska

I am now sold on the value

Lee, I was skeptical about the value of the College Launch Solution when I first heard about it. After all, I already have several of your other products and I'm a Gold Care Club member. You have been such a blessing, giving me the advice I need each week. My husband has been really impressed, too. But thanks to your emails, I have watched all three of your videos (leading up to the live webinar), and I am now sold on the value of the College Launch Solution!

Thank you for offering a Teen Track! Our two current high schoolers need to hear directly from you. Your "10

Critical C's of College and Career Success" is outstanding. I want to hear more about developing an "elevator pitch" for each of our kids. And I want to hear more about using amazing words to make the college application essay stand out.

I have experienced so much fear and panic about homeschooling high school, especially because of the ongoing struggles with my health. **You have been the answer to my prayers for help.** Although I attended a public high school, my dad was my guidance counselor and college coach. You're right, we can do this!

~Kari in California

For more information about my **College Launch Solution**, go to:

www.CollegeLaunchSolution.com

Use Promo Code **cls75** at checkout to get $75 off the regular price

Also from The HomeScholar...

- The HomeScholar Guide to College Admission and Scholarships: Homeschool Secrets to Getting Ready, Getting in and Getting Paid (Book and Kindle Book)

- Setting the Records Straight - How to Craft Homeschool Transcripts and Course Descriptions for College Admission and Scholarships (Book and Kindle Book)

- Total Transcript Solution (Online Training, Tools and Templates)

- Comprehensive Record Solution (Online Training, Tools and Templates)

- Gold Care Club (Comprehensive Online Support and Training)

- High School Solution (Comprehensive Training, Tools, Resources, and Support)

- College Launch Solution (Comprehensive Training, Tools, Resources, and Support)

- Parent Training Classes (Online Training)

The HomeScholar Coffee Break Books Released or Coming Soon on Kindle and Paperback:

- Delight Directed Learning: Guiding Your Homeschooler Toward Passionate Learning

- Creating Transcripts for Your Unique Child: Help Your Homeschool Graduate Stand Out from the Crowd

- Beyond Academics: Preparation for College and for Life

- Planning High School Courses: Charting the Course Toward High School Graduation

- Graduate Your Homeschooler in Style: Make Your Homeschool Graduation Memorable

- Keys to High School Success: Get Your Homeschool High School Started Right!

- Getting the Most Out of Your Homeschool This Summer: Learning just for the Fun of it!

- Finding a College: A Homeschooler's Guide to Finding a Perfect Fit

- College Scholarships for High School Credit: Learn and Earn With This Two-for-One Strategy!

- College Admission Policies Demystified: Understanding Homeschool Requirements for Getting In

- A Higher Calling: Homeschooling High School for Harried Husbands (by Matt Binz, Mr. HomeScholar)

- Gifted Education Strategies for Every Child: Homeschool Secrets for Success

- College Application Essays: A Primer for Parents

- Creating Homeschool Balance: Find Harmony Between Type A and Type Zzz...

- Homeschooling the Holidays: Sanity Saving Strategies and Gift Giving Ideas

- Your Goals this Year: A Year by Year Guide to Homeschooling High School

- Making the Grades: A Grouch-Free Guide to Homeschool Grading

- High School Testing: Knowledge That Saves Money

- Getting the BIG Scholarships: Learn Expert Secrets for Winning College Cash!

- Easy English for Simple Homeschooling: How to Teach, Assess and Document High School English

- Scheduling - The Secret to Homeschool Sanity: Plan You Way Back to Mental Health

- Junior Year is the Key to High School Success: How to Unlock the Gate to Graduation and Beyond

- Upper Echelon Education: How to Gain Admission to Elite Universities

- How to Homeschool College: Save Time, Reduce Stress and Eliminate Debt

- Homeschool Curriculum That's Effective and Fun: Avoid the Crummy Curriculum Hall of Shame!

- Comprehensive Homeschool Records: Put Your Best Foot Forward to Win College Admission and Scholarships

- Options After High School: Steps to Success for College or Career

- How to Homeschool 9th and 10th Grade: Simple Steps for Starting Strong!

- Senior Year Step-by-Step: Simple Instructions for Busy Homeschool Parents

- High School Math The Easy Way: Simple Strategies for Homeschool Parents in Over Their Heads

- Homeschooling Middle School with Powerful Purpose: How to Successfully Navigate 6th through 8th Grades

- Simple Science for Homeschooling High School: Because Teaching Science Isn't Rocket Science

- How to be Your Child's Best College Coach: Strategies for Success Using

Teens You'll Find Lying Around the House

Would you like to be notified when we offer the next *Coffee Break Books* for FREE during our Kindle promotion days? If so, leave your name and email at the link below and we will send you a reminder.

www.HomeHighSchoolHelp.com/ freekindlebook

Visit my Amazon Author Page!

amazon.com/author/leebinz

Made in the USA
San Bernardino, CA
14 December 2018